# Living Alone
# And Loving It

To Lavona,
Thanks for being
my friend.
Laurian

# Living Alone And Loving It

## A Practical and Philosophical Guide

## Laurian Harshman

**To order additional copies of this book, contact:**
Xlibris Corporation
1-888-795-4274
www.Xlibris.com
Orders@Xlibris.com
86877

# CONTENTS

ACKNOWLEDGMENTS ....................................................................7

INTRODUCTION.........................................................................9

TO JACK....................................................................................11

A NEW LIFE.............................................................................13

DEFINE YOURSELF.................................................................18

GET ORGANIZED.....................................................................25

FINANCIAL MATTERS .............................................................30

DAILY LIVING..........................................................................37

MOVING....................................................................................49

PREPARING TO COOK ............................................................54

COOKING AND EATING.........................................................60

FAMILY AND FRIENDS ..........................................................64

GETTING AWAY .......................................................................71

DATING .....................................................................................76

CONCLUSION ...........................................................................80

# ACKNOWLEDGMENTS

A big hug and many thanks to all the people whose stories and philosophies I used in this book, especially, but not limited to, Beatrice Atwater, Keith Netteburg, Kathy Pile, Earl (Mac) McCartney, Kathy Fiero, Kaye Willis, Joan Hohn, Kris Hansen, and Barbara Traister. To my daughter Katherine Sigler accolades for always believing in my writings. Finally, to Joe Mierzwa, huge thanks for your edits, suggestions, and help to make the publishing of this book possible.

**This book is dedicated to all the Barbaras in my life**

**Those here, there and gone.**
**Thank you all for your encouragement, love, and friendship.**

# INTRODUCTION

According to the U. S. Census Bureau, over thirty million Americans live alone. A third of them are young people less than age forty-five, who have not yet married, or for other reasons, involuntarily or voluntarily, live alone. The rest, some 20 million (a number which keeps growing as our population lives longer) are people over forty-five.

The purpose of this book is to help individuals who have lived all or most of their lives with another person and, because of the death of a companion, are faced with the often difficult prospect of living alone. The philosophical and practical suggestions were compiled from my own experiences and interviews with men and women who have lived alone, some for only a short time and others for years. Although the ideas to follow are intended for older individuals, young people who live alone and are responsible for all of life's intricacies without the help, suggestions, or hindrances of another may also benefit.

Some readers will be blessed with plenty of assets or income and can afford to do almost anything they want. Others may have limited monetary resources, perhaps only Social Security, with little or no discretionary income. Most of us fall somewhere in between the two extremes.

Some readers will already be doing, or know how to do, the activities and possess the attitudes described. Others may not have a clue about where to begin taking care of themselves, or how to work toward a fulfilled, even happy, life using their own special resources. Again, most of us fall somewhere in between.

The suggestions included in this work, both practical and philosophical, are merely that—suggestions that are based upon my experience and that of others who live by themselves. I hope, however, that even if you reject the practical, you will embrace the philosophical. There will be times as you read this book that you will say to yourself that you already do some of the activities, or that you do them more frequently or less often, or better, or don't want to do them at all. Okay. If only one or two of these ideas help you to navigate through a difficult time to a pleasurable life, I will have my reward.

In order to demonstrate an attitude or activity, I have included some of the results of my interviews with people who live alone, as well as some circumstances I encountered when I handled trusts and estates for a bank. I have not used real names for any of these people in order to protect their privacy.

Also, at the end of each chapter, I have included a thought to remember as you work towards living a satisfying life alone. The first thought is below:

**My thoughts influence my feelings. My feelings determine my actions and/or reactions. In other words, positive actions are a result of positive thoughts. I will keep my thoughts positive, even if I have to work hard to keep my glass more than half full instead of half empty.**

# *TO JACK*

*How can I say how much I shall miss you, my Jacque, my friend, my love. There are so many things we did and planned to share in the future.*

*How can I rise in the morning if there is no smell of coffee, no rustle of the paper, no cough to pull me from my slumber to sit and read the paper across from you. How will I know the funny tidbits you always read to me, that I never seemed to see.*

*I'll never again hear the door slam at noon or your cheery "lunchtime" calling me from my computer up the stairs to share your sometimes weird concoctions of cheese and ketchup and pickles on a cracker, and the happenings of your day. I'll miss the shoot-em-up westerns you always chose to watch on television, though for the most part you fell asleep while I learned more about John Wayne than I ever wanted to know.*

*No more will I receive the always thoughtful gifts or share our dinners out on our birthdays and anniversaries, or Christmas, times you never forgot. No more the plant on Easter or the "little something" on Mother's Day, even though I kept telling you I wasn't your mother.*

*Already I long to hear your silly sayings and play on words that I heard a thousand times, grew tired of, and now, so soon, can't remember.*

*Oh, Jocko, I never learned to tie that fishing knot, or run the motor on the boat. We'll never again sit in the middle of a lake, soaking up the sunshine and the beauty of the mountains, not caring if the fish were biting, enjoying each other's company, not saying much. No one else will want to turn off on some remote back road, or explore some ghost town or mine, or go four-wheel-driving over some incredibly beautiful, almost impassable pass, laughing when we reached to top to find a paved road going down the other side. No more will we make Swedish potato sausage together, for you somehow made a better Swede than I. And who will fix my screens and scrub my whitewall tires and keep my knives from going dull?*

*We'll never build that house in Grand Lake, never live in the mountains like we planned; never go camping again, struggling to put up the tent; never take that cruise to Alaska; never put on our sweats, build a fire, and "mosey in" when it snows; never do all the things we talked about, hoping, laughing, when and if I sold my first book.*

*I mourn for our grandchildren, for Robbie who has talked all winter about going fishing with his Papa. I mourn for Kevin who looks so much like you and will never remember you at all. I mourn for Tiffany who received her Varsity letter in track the night you died and never got to share it with you. You would have been so pleased and proud.*

*I mourn for your daughter, Pam, whom I know you loved so very much and never told. For my children, Kathy and David, who were as much your children as if they had been your own.*

*I mourn for us all, for we never learned the secret of your incredible fried chicken.*

*Go with God, my husband. You were my lover, my confidante, my companion, but most of all my friend. I cherish every year, every single minute we had together. And someday, somewhere, we'll share it all again.*

# A NEW LIFE

Losing your companion may seem like the end of your world. In a way, it is. It is the end of the chapter of life where one's identity is defined as part of a team as well as an individual. Whether you had a difficult or a happy relationship; whether you spent most of the time enjoying activities together or apart, there was someone in your household to care about, to talk with, to laugh with, and to plan for the future. The grief you feel is often not only that your partner's life has ended, but also that you now must live and make decisions by yourself.

It was comforting to me to find there is no right or wrong way to grieve. One person I interviewed for this book said she did not cry at all and was determined to carry on as if she had lived alone all her life. Another said she cried for days and could not function for weeks. Some people talk incessantly of their partner; others never mention him or her. One friend said as soon as the funeral was over, she booked a cruise around the world. Apparently, her husband never wanted to travel and she did. She was determined to see the world while she could. Personally, I was furious with my husband for dying so young when we had such wonderful plans for retirement. In short, whatever you are feeling, or however you handle your sadness is not wrong. It may be just different from what someone else would do.

As soon as the first shock and grieving begins to diminish, it is time to realize that one chapter of your life is completed and to embrace the fact that you now have the opportunity to plan for and live a new interesting, even exciting, life. A new era has begun!

I remember the evening after my husband died, I sat silently on the living room sofa staring into space, with my shoulders slumped, my lips trembling, tears sliding down to my chin, already lonely, wondering how I could cope with living without Jack. My daughters talked quietly across from me.

"At least," my older daughter said, laughing and catching my attention. "There's one good thing. We won't have to eat 'mock ham salad" ever again."

"You mean that awful bologna and cheese spread that Dad loved?" my other daughter laughed. "You're right. That is a **good** thing."

"And we can eat popcorn with our fingers instead of with a spoon," I offered. We all laughed and went on, with more laughter, to recount more of my husband's other funny eccentricities. I cherish that moment of laughter and now realize even when life seems the darkest, we can and need to laugh. And we need to share our laughter and our lives with people who care about us.

**Living alone does not mean lonely living**. Remember this. Instead, living alone means freedom, within legal and ethical restraints, to do the things we want to do, and when and how we want to do them. It means we can eat what and when we want, smile and have fun when we can, have our own opinions without debate, and the time to accomplish our own desires. Living alone means the opportunity to pursue what we do well and love, and to learn new tasks which have not been our responsibility in the past.

Dealing with life is about choices. We cannot control everything that happens in our lives, but we can control how we react and how we feel. We can choose to enjoy life, to remember past good times, *and* we can choose to view reverses as challenges. To be contented with life is to be focused on what we do have and not on what we don't have, or the past. If we strive to be positive about whatever life brings us, we can find contentment, even happiness.

Several years ago, when I was a trust officer for a bank, I was assigned two customers whose husbands died at about the same time. Both women, Mona and Eleanor, were in their mid-seventies, had no children, and were in good health. Neither woman had been responsible for handling finances or investments, so their husbands had established trusts to assure financial stability for their wives.

I soon discovered Mona was not handling life well without her husband. She refused to go out of her house, so if I needed to discuss the trust or her necessities, I had to visit her at home. The house was a mess, she was often still in her nightgown when I arrived, her hair was not combed, she wore no makeup, and her answers to my questions were peppered with complaints. After a particularly disturbing visit, I hired a companion for Mona to prepare meals and keep the house clean. In a month or so, the companion told me Mona refused to take baths and had to be forced to go to the bathroom and often eliminated in her bed or chair. Obviously, Mona was severely depressed, but would not allow me to seek professional help for her. Every time I went to see her, she said over and over that she had nothing to live for and just wanted to die. And a few months later, she did.

Eleanor came to see me at the bank a few days after her husband died. She wanted to make sure that she would be able to sell her house and move into a retirement community. I assured her from a financial standpoint she could and that I would help her with the process. From that time on, we met regularly, often going out for lunch when she would tell me of her latest trip, or the myriad of cocktail parties she had hosted or gone to. She told me about the latest plays and musicals she had seen, and related hilarious happenings of her many friends. She was always dressed beautifully and there was a sparkle in her eye. Our professional relationship grew into friendship. One day we were scheduled to go to lunch and she didn't show up. Finally, I called the retirement community office and was told that Eleanor had died the night before.

Which life would you choose?

The path to physical or mental recovery can be painful. Remember how a cut or abrasion itches as it heals? And how continually scratching the sore keeps it from healing or makes it worse? A physical hurt needs to be consciously endured and not scratched in order to heal. Likewise, the pain of losing your partner is part of the healing process. Your pain needs to be acknowledged, but not enhanced or made worse by constantly dwelling on your loss.

Learning to live alone is merely one more change in life—like graduating from high school or college; getting married; having a baby; changing or losing a job; moving to a new house or city; sending your youngest off to college; or retiring. There will be new things to learn, challenges to overcome, setbacks, triumphs, sadness and joy. Expect some reversals, but vow to forge ahead with a smile. You can deal with this change with the same fortitude you had for life's other challenges. If you are saying to yourself that you didn't do so well with change in the past, now is the time to **dive right in!** Upgrade your attitude to positive, and pursue happiness.

Recent scientific studies have shown that people who are caring and compassionate; who surround themselves with friends and family, who keep busy with activities that are interesting to them, and who have a positive attitude about life and others, live longer, have better health, recover from adversity more quickly, and live contented, even happy lives. So, even if you have not always practiced these attributes, start now.

How? By reaching out to those you know and to new friends with sincere interest and compassion; that is, by sincerely sympathizing with others' circumstances and pain, by having empathy with their successes, failures and daily life. By keeping up with the activities of an orderly daily life, and by finding new ones that you look forward to doing. By doing away with anger at others for happenings that are really your fault, or that they didn't mean, but that you perceived as hurtful. By choosing to laugh or turn to "Plan B" when things outside of or within your control go wrong. By being comfortable that your surroundings, activities, and friends are of your own choosing.

Everyone has problems, reverses and pain. Most problems are about health, money, relationships, having time to get everything done, unexpected repairs and expenses for your home or your car, or the loss of a loved one. Or the problem can be as simple as trying to take the lid off a jar. The way we deal with problems makes the difference between being contented and happy, and being miserable. All too often, when something goes wrong, we find someone or something to blame. We criticize, we get angry, we dwell on our unhappiness, we puff the incident all out of proportion, and sometimes we sue. Does any of this negative behavior make us feel better? Probably not. Negative thoughts and behavior can make a problem worse.

Instead of negative behaviors when something goes wrong, ask yourself if you created the problem or contributed to it in some way. Then, instead of blaming someone else, define the problem. Determine if you can solve it, and, if so, take responsibility for doing so, either by yourself or with help. If a problem is beyond your control, minimize your anguish. Tell yourself that it won't matter in a hundred years anyway, forget it as best you can, and move on to some positive endeavor. And try a smile or laughter, whenever you can. Say to yourself:

**What my life will be is up to me**

# DEFINE YOURSELF

When we lose a loved one who has been a part of our life for a long time, it can be difficult to remember our own self worth. We tend to think of ourselves as part of a couple, as a team, and to forget we are valuable in our own right as part of society and to the people we know. It is important to begin right away to identify who we are, so we can enhance and cherish the talents and interests which will enable us to lead a fulfilling life by ourselves.

Before we explore how to live an enjoyable life alone, I want you to consider a question a friend asked me: "What do you think influenced your philosophy of life?"

A great question. I had to confess I didn't know the answer. Nevertheless, the question consumed my thinking for several days. What circumstances or people had influenced my philosophy?

Before I could determine what influenced my outlook on life, I discovered I had to define who I am. I concluded that I am an optimist who, after studying and organizing an endeavor, expects things to go right. I often have Plan B, and generally don't worry about what can go wrong. When I encounter reverses or problems, I try to solve them as best as I can and then I move on. I am an introvert, meaning I love to read and write and cook more than any other endeavors, but push myself to be gregarious and a good friend. I have strong opinions as long as I have time to think. I am a good listener. I love to laugh.

What influenced my thinking? How much influence on my life did having parents who were not only loving, but who took the time to encourage me to always be the best that I can? Did it happen when as a 13-year-old I complained that I was too tall and too fat and unpopular, my mother made me write a list of my grievances beside another list of the good things in my life? And the good things outnumbered the bad? Did I become an optimist because my first child died after a day, but I went on to have two healthy children? Or when, in my early twenties, my grandmother and my parents all died and my first husband was diagnosed with multiple sclerosis, so I had to rely on myself to provide for my two children, my younger brother, and an ill husband? Could it be that losing my support system at a young age prepared me for the death of my second husband, Jack, and my son, and my younger brother? Did my success in the business world and listening to many motivational speakers over the years contribute to my attitude? Just how much influence did my marriage to Jack and our sharing of so many good times contribute to my sense of always being lucky?

When I went back to people I had already interviewed and asked these questions, I was pleasantly surprised at their thoughtful and often lengthy answers. Most of the writings included the person's life history and challenges. I want those who took the time to review their lives and who they are to know I treasure their answers. In all but one case, when they handed me their writings, they thanked me for asking them to think about who they were and how their lives were influenced and conducted by others and circumstances.

Following is a synopsis of those introspections. Please note that I have not used real names and, in the interest of brevity, I have paraphrased answers or used selected quotes. The people who contributed their thoughts will no doubt recognize what they wrote and I apologize if I have not captured the essence of who they are.

As you read through their answers, please be thinking about your own philosophy and your life, so that at the end of the chapter, you can fill in the space I left for this purpose. Then, as you read the rest of the book, you should be better prepared to either enhance or change your thinking to lead a fulfilling life.

All but one of the people who answered the question about who they are said they are optimists. The pessimist said she always expects things to go wrong and constantly worries about what will happen next. The optimists said they expected life to be good and didn't worry about circumstances beyond their control that could go wrong.

<u>Mary:</u> I used to be a pessimist, but my faith in God and his blessings have taught me to be optimistic because everything turns out for the best. Being a Christian does not take away problems, but it gives me a positive perspective to deal with them.

I have had a hard life but a good life. My biological mother had polio and couldn't take care of me, so I was raised by foster parents. At the age of three, I was diagnosed with cerebral palsy and, over the years, had four operations on my legs, but still have difficulty walking. Nevertheless, because I was taught to be independent, I lived by myself and worked until my recent retirement. I handle each problem as it comes up and take reverses in stride.

<u>Sam:</u> I am an optimist and usually expect everything to be okay. I am not much of a worrier and try to handle problems as they arise by analyzing the situation, finding the cause, and then trying to find a solution. I set goals and select a reasonable time to complete them. I now conduct my life by continuing the habits I developed during my 27 years in the military and in my second career as an educator in a community college.

During my careers, I selected role models. These were people who conducted their lives in a way that I admired and could emulate. Modeling myself after other good people helped me to learn that it is better to say nothing than to lie, to always to do my best at every task, and to always be on time if possible.

<u>Doris:</u> I'm old enough to know life will have money and health challenges, but I expect all problems to be solved eventually. Life isn't a hand-out; if you want some control and satisfaction and joy, you have to participate.

My parents had difficult health problems and not much money. Nevertheless, they let me know that they loved and supported me. The unspoken message was "Keep on. Do not give up. You can figure it out. You can do it. We know you can."

I believe what we do and think has a ripple effect on nearby people, our location in the world, and the earth itself. Good thoughts and actions by even one person can change the world.

People are people. Accept people as they are or get them out of your life. Remember, the only person who can change a person's attitude is that person, not anyone else.

Polly: I strive to be responsible and trustworthy with a healthy mind for learning and growth. I generally expect things to go right, but when I encounter problems, I write them down, think them over, sometimes discuss them with my sons, and decide what to do. It is my desire to be worthwhile and to set a good example for my children.

My parents, my sons, and my numerous jobs have influenced my life. My parents taught me work ethics, honor, and independence. My sons taught me to be flexible with their generation. My various jobs, now and over the years, taught me flexibility and, oh, yes, that I don't know it all.

Rick: I think of myself as a recovered pessimist. At this point in my life, I love my work and look forward to solving whatever challenges life may bring. I love my two children and my grandchildren. I seldom miss a golf game with the guys. I like to travel and enjoy a good laugh whenever I can. You might say I love my life. It wasn't always so.

My father was a plumber, and now that I think about it, an entrepreneur. During the time I was growing up, he hired other plumbers and his business became a well known citywide company. When I told him I wanted to go to college and become a geologist, he said no. Since I was the only son, he demanded I learn to be a plumber who could take over his business when he retired. I hated plumbing, I think I hated my father, and felt miserable. I was very pessimistic about life in general.

My father died in a car accident when I was twenty-five. I hate to say it, but his passing changed my life. With my mother's blessing. I sold my father's business. The sale provided my mother with an income and I was able to go to college and earn my master's degree in geology. I married, have a daughter and a son, who have both gone to college, and have great jobs and families. When my wife died of cancer last year, it was hard because we shared so much together, but I have adjusted to living alone. I look forward to retirement in a year or so and plan to offer my services as a teacher.

Betsy: For the most part, I expect things to go right, although at times I look at the worst case scenario and worry about it even though I don't expect it to happen. Maybe such concerns are because I am a lawyer.

As far as handling problems, I think I have never had any *real* problems. My husband never even looked at another woman. My five children were basically problem free when they were growing up. They all have good educations and lead productive lives. I have always been healthy and expect to be healthy. I have always had enough financially and have never gone hungry. I feel fortunate that I was born in the USA and to grow up in the American west. I do have a few regrets, but since I can't change the past, there is no use dwelling on them.

Ann: Yup, I am an optimist. Each stage of life is a learning experience. I know it isn't up to someone else to make me happy or successful; it is up to me. I try to be independent, to learn how to do things for myself, and not rely on someone else to do it for me. I've learned if I try to do something and it doesn't work out, it is not failure, it is a learning experience.

Life isn't perfect. Everyone has problems, makes mistakes, and has bad times. Life does not come with a guarantee to be easy without heartache or always what we want. My philosophy it that no matter what happens, it will work out and is for the best. I focus on what I can do and what I have rather than on what I can't do or don't have. Even though I am alone now, I thank God for my loving family and the lessons they taught me.

Cynthia: Sometimes it is a struggle to be an optimist, although it has become easier as I get older. "Why worry?" I say to myself. "Will it help the situation? Will it make me feel better? No. It will be whatever it will be." My life has been full to brim with problems and reverses, but it is also full of blessings and happiness, so why focus on the negative.

I am possibly a bit unique in that there are people in my life that influenced my behavior and beliefs by learning from them how not to act or live. My mother taught me to work hard, but she also taught me how not to be a parent. I spent my childhood telling myself I would never treat my children the way she treated me. I hope my children would agree that I have been a good parent.

I divorced my first husband who taught me how I should not treat other people. His attitude gave me direction for who I truly want to be, and the strength to stand up for myself, my children, and my future.

The point of my telling you about my soul searching and that of others is to encourage you to do the same. Before you read the rest of this book, take the time to define and jot down on the pages that follow who you are, how you have handled life, and what circumstances or people may have influenced your philosophy.

**Though I am what I am**
**I can strive to do better**

What is your philosophy of life?

Who or what influenced your thinking?

# GET ORGANIZED

Whether you have lived alone for a short or a long time, you need to make your home and your life yours. That is, not a left over life from when you lived with a partner or family.

As soon as the funeral is over, you need to take action. Do not delay. Procrastination will sink you into mind-numbing self pity. Action will keep your mind off your loss and will lead to self-satisfaction.

First, on the lighter side, action does not mean rushing out to buy six new black dresses or suits. In the past, and still in some cultures, it was the custom for surviving spouse, particularly a woman, to wear black or a black armband for a year after a spouse died. Now, while it shows a sign of respect to wear black to the funeral, it is no longer necessary for widows (or widowers) to wear black on a daily basis. In fact, limiting yourself to dreary garb will dampen your spirits and continually remind others that you are alone.

Your first action, instead, should be to notify friends, family, credit card companies, your bank, your attorney, your accountant and anyone else of importance, that you are now single and entirely responsible for your financial affairs. If necessary, provide death certificates or other documentation.

Next, get rid of your partner's clothes, jewelry and other belongings. This activity was one of the hardest things I have ever had to do because felt I was betraying Jack by giving away his belongings. The problem with keeping these possessions for any period of time is that every time you open a closet full of your partner's clothes, or see her jewelry box or perfume, or his golf clubs, you will be reminded of your loss. If you retain only a few special things, you can minimize the number of times "things" remind you of your loss. I kept one of my husband's rings which I wear often on my index finger. When I put it on, I think of Jack, but it no longer makes me sad.

Going through and discarding a partner's belongings is best done right away while you can enlist the aid of family or friends who are available now but will soon return to their own lives. Try not to go through your partner's things by yourself; it is far too depressing without another's perspective, and besides, you will have a tendency to keep too many things for sentimental reasons, only to pitch them out later. When tempted to keep something, other than pictures or mementos, as hard as it may seem, keep reminding yourself that your partner is **not** coming back.

Adult children, if available, are the best help for the job of ridding your household of your partner's belongings, but if they live far away or are too busy, or you have no children, enlist the aid of one or more of your spouse's friends. Let your friends and family take what they want, give reusable items to charity or hold a garage sale, and sell collections, either on the Internet or to an antique dealer. Dispose of all your partner's medications. Don't, however, give away items such as dishes or tools you can use.

Note that many charities or assisted living homes will welcome such items as wheel chairs, crutches or other medical devices in good condition. Give or sell these items if you cannot reasonably expect that you will need them in a year or so.

After separating your partner's items from yours, take the opportunity to organize your surroundings in ways that are most convenient and pleasing to you. Since there will be more room in the closet, spread out your clothes, scrutinize each item, and give away anything you have not worn or used for more than two or three years. Use extra drawers and shelves to put away items that before had no place of their own.

Everyone organizes a kitchen in the way that makes the most sense to that person. Think about what you like about your kitchen and what you don't; then, unless the existing organization pleases you, change it. Put glasses, silverware and dishes where they are most accessible; pans and foodstuffs in larger cabinets. Take the opportunity to throw out or give away dishes and food you don't like, or is outdated. Add small pans for cooking for one, but keep large ones for family visits and entertaining.

As soon as you have completed organizing your kitchen, look around the rest of your home. Do you want to keep that old leather chair that matches nothing, but that your deceased husband loved? Do you really like the flowered sofa or the rocking chair where your wife did her knitting? Have you always hated the color of the bedroom, but couldn't change it because it was your spouse's favorite color? Give away the chair, recover or replace the sofa, move furniture around to make the layout more pleasing, and paint the walls, depending, of course, on what you can afford. If you think you might move sometime soon, you may want to wait to make big changes, but even little changes will be satisfying. *Caution!* Don't give away your freezer. As you will see later on in the chapters about food, you will need extra freezer space more than ever.

Living alone may mean you may have to learn to take care of household chores that you were not responsible for before your partner left you. For instance, when I interviewed Susan, she said, "The hardest thing I had to learn after Rick died was how to put gas in the lawnmower. I finally gave up and hired my neighbor's son to mow the lawn." Similarly, George, a widower in his 80's confessed, "If I had known how much time housework takes and that it can sometimes be complicated, I would have helped my wife more."

Learning to take care of your self by yourself will take time, just like any new experience. There are a myriad of things you can do to make your life safe and easier. Here are a few to consider:

— Put a telephone next to your bed where you can reach it easily.
— If you have health or mobility problems, consider an emergency beeper that you wear all the time.
— Purchase a cell phone and carry it with you at all times when you are away from home, or, as an increasing number of people are doing to save telephone costs, use a cell phone exclusively for all calls and cancel your regular home service.

— Obtain a sturdy step ladder for high-to-reach places.
— Build accessible shelves in the garage or basement or closets; then place infrequently used decorations and other items in boxes, label them on the ends, preferably with a black marking pen, and store the boxes on the shelves.
— Buy rolling garbage cans so you don't have to carry those old heavy ones out to the street.
— Attach easy clasps to your jewelry (this is a big frustration to women with long finger nails, poor eyesight and no husband).
— Find a flexible rubber gripper to open jars.
— Keep a magnifying glass in the medicine cabinet so you can read that insanely small print on medicine containers.
— Put night lights in the hall and in your bathroom so you can find your way easily if you have to get up during the night. If you are afraid of the dark, you can put a night light in your bedroom, although some say this may interfere with sleeping well.
— Put chain locks on your doors, and, depending on where you live, consider a security system.

You don't have to make your home yours all at once, but do it soon. If you are working, it will take longer, but will fill your weekends, when many people who live alone find the hardest time. If you are physically unable, or don't want to make changes on your own, hire a handyman or some willing trustworthy person to help. Or consider having a "grandparent weekend" to enlist the aid of your children and/or grandchildren.

There may be times when your grief will overtake your determination to make your home yours. When this happens, stop sorting, go for a walk, watch a comedy on TV, read a book, or go out to dinner, either alone or with a friend. When you feel better, go back to the task. Making your home the way you want it will keep your spirits up in the long run. Don't be like one of my neighbors who refused to go down into the basement where her deceased husband's tools and hobbies were kept, and merely pushed his clothes to the back of the closet, even though he had been dead for over ten years. The cleanup problem, she said, would be her nephew's when she died.

When I completed the organization of my home, I found a sense of empowerment. I couldn't bring my husband back, but I could control my surroundings. I vowed to keep it that way by putting things in their place after use. And, for the most part, I have kept that vow, though I have to admit that sometimes the papers on my desk tend to pile up. It takes so little time to keep your surroundings neat, and the lift a clean, organized home will give you is certainly worth the time. Nothing is more depressing (for me at least) than coming home to an unmade bed, dirty dishes in the sink, or papers all over the floor in every room. A word of caution, though. Don't become obsessed with housework; make sure you leave plenty of time for all the things that make life pleasurable.

**To avoid being traumatized**
**I vow to keep my home organized.**

# FINANCIAL MATTERS

When I mentioned to an accountant friend that I was writing this book, he told me the following story. Without revealing her name to me, he said he met a client in a grocery store. When he sent his regards to her husband, she sadly replied, "My husband died. Didn't you know?" Thinking the death must have been recent, and that he would like to attend the funeral, he asked about the arrangements. "What arrangements?" she replied. "He died six months ago. I guess only my family knows, since I have been too depressed and upset to tell anyone else." He replied that he was sorry for her loss and then offered to send copies of her tax returns and any other financial information to her attorney. "What attorney?" she replied. "Why would I need an attorney? Anyway, my husband handled all that financial stuff. I don't know anything about it."

"What did you do?" I asked.

He sighed. "With her permission, I contacted her attorney, who knew her husband's stock broker. The three of us reconstructed her husband's estate and helped her as executrix to probate the will and file the necessary estate and income tax returns. Unfortunately, she had no children. If she had, our job might have been easier."

The foregoing illustration points out that concurrent with making your home yours is the vitally important task of organizing your financial affairs. As soon as possible, no more than a few days after losing your partner, you need to go through your papers, safe deposit box, home safe, and other records. Whether or not you find a will, call your attorney, your broker, if any, and your accountant. Death is both a legal and often taxable event requiring the help and advice of an attorney as well as other financial experts. If you don't have legal counsel, ask a trusted family member or friend for a referral.

Next, segregate all other documents such as marriage certificates, divorce papers, birth certificates, passports, bank account information, IRA records, Social Security entitlements, stocks, bonds, savings accounts, pension notices and insurance documents into labeled files. Become familiar with all your financial records, know where to find them, and be careful about shredding documents you think are no longer relevant until later when you are sure of their irrelevance. Of course, if you are the person who always paid all the bills and filed tax returns and are meticulous about keeping records, this chore may be easier. On the other hand, if you have never been the financial person, you need to learn and learn fast. Consider asking a friend to recommend a financial and/or tax advisor, if you don't already have these, but only take the advice of someone you trust implicitly.

Every single person needs to know his or her financial position. This can be determined by asking questions like:

— What are my assets? Did my spouse and I have stocks, bonds, real estate, or nothing?
— Did my spouse have a 401(k) retirement plan or IRA? Do I?
— Did my spouse have a pension that terminated? Will I be entitled to that pension or some portion of it?
— Am I entitled to Social Security? Is it better to take my spouse's Social Security or my own?
— What is my current income? What income, if any, can I expect in the future?
— Can I afford the place where I live now, or the car I drive? If not, what can I afford?

If you are still working, consider adding as much of your income as possible to a 401(k) retirement account, or Individual Retirement Account (IRA). The more you contribute to these tax deferred accounts, the better off you will be when you finally retire. At first, these funds may be invested in savings, but when you have accumulated over five thousand dollars, consider diversifying your holdings. Except for savings, it is not a good idea to invest in only one stock or bond or real estate. This is why mutual funds are popular, and it is often a good idea to spread your investments into several funds, instead of only one. A trustworthy investment advisor can help you with this.

**Caution!** Never give money or other assets to someone who solicits your business. And, if someone offers you an investment which yields more than average market rates and sounds too good to be true, it probably is. There are hundreds, maybe thousands, of scam artists who prey on older, uninformed, financially naive people, especially those who have suffered the loss of a loved one and who may be vulnerable.

If you are left with the proceeds of a large insurance policy, the temptation may be to buy a new car or house, or go on an extended vacation that you wouldn't otherwise be able to afford. Wait! There are important considerations to make. Should you pay off your mortgage or credit cards or the car loan? Or would the funds be better off invested, so that you can retain the mortgage write-off, and afford to retire comfortably? My purpose is not to tell you what to do with your assets and income, but only to alert you that you need to have good advice, take slow steps, and use caution while planning your financial future. And to suggest that, even if you have an extensive background in finance or investing, always consult someone else, at least for a time. All too often when we think we know it all, we make mistakes because we are involved emotionally and do not have an objective view of the situation.

If you have extensive assets and income, this is great. Realistically, however, many people find themselves with less income when left alone. Go through your checkbook and list all your expenditures, then compare that amount with your income. Ask yourself if you really need magazine subscriptions, newspapers, clothes, massages, a second car, or other items, that may be unused and unnecessary. Cancel or sell whatever you can. Put together a budget, even if it is rudimentary, so you can remain financially viable. If it appears your income will not be enough, it is all right, in most cases, to discuss this with your children. You may require their help.

On the other hand, be careful about loaning your children money without legal advice and a written contract. My aunt, after her husband died, loaned her son a substantial down payment to buy a home. She trusted him and felt he would repay the loan, so did not require him or his wife sign a loan agreement. For two years, the son made monthly payments to her. Then, when he son was killed in an automobile accident, his wife refused to repay the loan, saying she knew nothing about the loan, and in any case, there was no loan contract. My aunt was devastated. Default of the loan affected where and how she lived for the rest of her life.

Be cautious about discussing your financial matters with friends. Most cannot (or will not) help you and really, for the most part, it is none of their business. For instance, a trust customer of mine confided she had told a friend of her late husband about an insurance policy she inherited. He proceeded to tell her about a stock he had recently purchased. Thinking he was recommending that she also invest in that stock, she used the entire proceeds of the policy to buy it. Later, the price of the stock dropped substantially and she lost about one-half of the value. Later, she found that the friend had only a small holding in this risky stock as part of a well-diversified portfolio so that the loss didn't affect him much. "Thank heavens," she told me, "my husband has the foresight to establish a trust for me with our other assets. I guess he knew I don't have much sense when it comes to finances."

It is important to keep certain records, such as receipts, bank statements, closing costs for your home, and other documents as well as tax returns and income statements. Some documents, like deeds, birth certificates, death certificates, passports, and contracts should be kept in a fire proof cabinet or a safe deposit box. Documentation for tax deductions, income and bank statements, and other receipts can be filed in an expanding file or in files for each purpose, or, if you are as lazy as I am, in a drawer in my desk, to be sorted out at tax time.

At the end of this chapter, I have included a time table for retention of documents for tax purposes. I suggest you copy this list and keep it with your tax returns or retain it on your computer. Please also consult your tax advisor.

Pay your bills on time. Penalties and interest are expensive and you need a good credit rating. Establish a routine of paying bills and taking care of other paperwork at least twice a month, or more frequently, if needed. Pay off credit cards every month if you can, but if not, as soon as possible.

Don't buy "stuff" just because it's cheap or you like it. If you question what you will use something for, or if you will eat it soon, and the answer is negative, put down the item and move on to the next. You will save money, your home won't be cluttered with "stuff", and your larder will contain only the food that you use.

Most importantly, acknowledge to yourself that your circumstances have changed, and even if you have a will, consider consulting your attorney to determine if you should write a new one. Think carefully about the people who will receive your estate and the consequences of your beneficence. For instance, during my banking career, I handled estates and trusts for people who named the bank as executor or trustee. I remember one woman who told me she thought her mother hadn't loved her. The mother left most of her estate to the woman's brother who was a drug addict and had never accomplished anything in his life, while the woman and her other brother were successful and had nice families. I knew that the mother thought her successful children didn't need her money and the errant brother did. The unintended consequence of her will rewarded bad behavior, ignored the good, and made two of her children feel unloved. The point is, try to make your provisions as equal as possible, even though you may feel sorry for one child or nephew or whoever. Remember that decisions based on emotion instead of on facts and equity might not be what you intend at all.

If you have personal things, like jewelry, that you want certain people to have, make a list that can be changed from time to time as you add or sell or give away items. Refer to the list in the will, or at least keep it with the will. Also make a list of insurance policies, addresses, bank accounts, safe deposit boxes, and all other financial items and keep it with a copy of your will.

Once you or your attorney have drawn your will and have signed and had it witnessed in accordance with the laws of your state, you should make copies. Leave one with your attorney, put the original in a fireproof box in your home or a safe deposit box, and, if it seems appropriate to you, give copies to the beneficiaries of the will. Destroy all old wills. Then, if you change your will in any way later, be sure to repeat the above process.

Also, if you do not want to be resuscitated and/or if you wish to be cremated, put these provisions in writing. Keep these documents with your will and discuss them with your family and trusted friends. Make sure you physician has a copy, too. Discussing such matters is often difficult, but you must remember it will be more difficult for your loved ones if they have to make these decisions without knowing your wishes.

**Paying bills and organizing records may not be fun,**
**But I look forward to relief when it's done.**

# RECORDS RENTENTION SCHEDULE*
*American Institute of Certified Public Accountants, Inc.

| ITEM | RENTION PERIOD |
| --- | --- |
| Accident Reports/claims | 7 years |
| Bankruptcy Documents | Permanently |
| Bank statements | 3 years |
| Canceled Checks (also see below) | 7 years |
| Canceled Checks for important payments, such as taxes, purchases of real or other property | Permanently |
| Contracts, mortgages, deeds, notes, leases, and bills of sale (expired) | 7 years |
| Contracts, etc. still in effect | Permanently |
| Correspondence, legal and important Important matters | Permanently |
| Insurance policies (expired) | 3 years |
| Insurance policies, records, claims | Permanently |
| Patents and related documents | Permanently |
| Property appraisals | Permanently |
| Retirement and pensions records | Permanently |
| Tax returns with worksheets, income reports and other relevant documentation | Permanently |
| Trademark and copy write registrations | Permanently |

# DAILY LIVING

All that paperwork, discarding, and organizing should keep you busy during the days and weeks after your loss, while simultaneously keeping you from dwelling on your partner's absence. You will probably feel pretty good about your accomplishments, but may at some point start wondering "Now what?" When you run out of the immediate undertakings, take several deep breaths, pat yourself on the back, and vow to keep your good habits. Then, establish *new* good habits and discard the attitudes and routines that will stop you from enjoying your life. Remember there are always plenty of activities to keep us busy, including daily maintenance, eating, and the really fun stuff.

The prospect of living alone every day, perhaps for the rest of one's life, is often the most disconcerting part of losing a partner. And from personal experience and talking with others, the first year is the hardest. You are used to having someone to talk with and share with, and even if that person was not well, you had someone else to care about. The way to keep your spirits up, to not fall into a depressing funk, is to decide what you want to do with the rest of your life. Set some goals, post them on the refrigerator, and vow to always look forward. I hasten to add, however, that it is okay and healthy to miss your partner, to cry a little at times, and to think of the adventures, conversations and disagreements you shared, but try to remember the past fondly without dwelling on it every minute. There is nothing we can do to change the past, but we *can* be grateful for good memories and we *can* determine our future. This is why it is important to know who we are, what our philosophy of life is, and what we want to do with the rest of our lives.

Chances are that prior to a partner's leaving or dying, you had a life that most of the time, or at least part of the time, did not include the presence of a partner. The trick is to enhance, add to, embellish, and, when necessary, change that previous life.

If you are working, continue. Even if you don't have to work for financial reasons, consider continuing to work as long as you can, retiring only by forced retirement, by health issues, or your preference. You will know the right time to quit. And then, when you terminate your full time employment, you might want to consider a part time job or establishing your own business—something you are good at and love.

If you don't have to or don't want to be gainfully employed, volunteer your time and expertise to an entity that offers services that you find interesting. For instance, retirement homes, senior centers, and hospitals generally welcome the help of volunteers. If you enjoy the arts, consider volunteering to usher at museums, art galleries, plays, or musicals. Political groups depend on volunteer constituents for support.

Volunteering doesn't appeal to you? Then take a class in painting or ceramics. Spend the winter months putting all those old pictures in albums. There are classes for creating interesting albums you might consider. Or put together a cookbook of your favorite recipes for your children or grandchildren. Take golf lessons and play golf as often as you want. Play tennis. If you are good at home maintenance, offer to help your neighbors with their maintenance problems. Become a mentor to a girl or boy who has lost a parent. Take computer classes. Buy books, get a library card, find a used book store, and read, read, read. Ski. Hike. Bird watch. Become a guide to local points of interest. The main thing is if you identify activities you can be passionate about, it will be easy to find worthy and interesting endeavors as you make your way through the rest of your life.

What if the loss of your partner means you do not have sufficient income to volunteer or pursue personal interests? My neighbor, Betty, was faced with this situation, but is the busiest person I know. When I called to ask if I could interview her for this book, she hesitated, then said she would have to consult her planner and would call me back.

When Betty finally called back that evening, she said, with a laugh, " I can fit you in for an hour so on Thursday afternoon at three o'clock. That is, if they don't call me to substitute teach."

She was called to teach, as it turned out, but we did manage to get together on a Sunday afternoon. My conversation with her revealed what an amazing person she is. She not only works as a substitute teacher as needed, but works two or three days a week at the convention center, teaches evening classes for adults twice a week, and ushers for matinee plays at the local county theatre. In between, she has lunches and dinners with friends, and takes one or two weeks off from all this activity several times a year to visit her children and grandchildren in another state. When I asked Betty if she liked to read, she said yes, but seldom did, because there was no time. "I think" she said "the reason I enjoy life so much is that I am so busy I have no time to be lonely or sad."

Working or volunteering has great benefits. Whether you have to work to live, or can donate your time, the associations with people, the routine of getting up and showing up, and the satisfaction of knowing you are needed are the most important rewards.

When you lived with another person, you probably had a morning routine. You got up, showered, shaved, fixed your hair, put on makeup, dressed, ate breakfast, read or watched the news, exercised, and planned your day. Not necessarily all or more of the foregoing, or in that order, but some kind of routine. Keep doing it, or establish a new regimen. It will be easy to say to yourself that no one will see you anyway, so why comb your hair, shave, or put on makeup? The answer is *you* see you when you pass a mirror, and if the person you see is disheveled and haggard it will be easy to give up trying for a satisfying life. Likewise, don't fall into the habit of sleeping until ten, or dragging around in your p.j.s all day. Such behavior will depress you and lead you to believe that your entire existence depended on your living with another.

While on the subject of morning routine, establish a habit of making your bed when you first get up. The bed will look neat for the rest of the day and you won't have this chore hanging over your head. Now that you are alone, you will probably sleep on only one side of the bed, so instead of folding down or taking off a bedspread or comforter, just fold it over the other side of the bed. Then in the morning, just pull up the sheet, and with a flick of your wrist, you can pull the folded half over your side and in an instant your bed is made! A comforter, of course, is the easiest of all. Just straighten the sheets, pull up the comforter, throw on a couple of decorative pillows and you're done.

Don't forget to wash towels at least once a week. Wash sheets at least every two weeks, if not more frequently. If you have two sets of sheets, strip the soiled one off and put on the second set right then. It takes only about ten minutes for the whole process and your reward for this simple chore is the uplifting feeling of clean sheets.

Exercise and diet are important to maintain your health, live longer, ward off decreased mental capacity, and look younger than you are.

Health: Schedule regular, at least annual, checkups with your health provider. There is no one to remind you to do this, so put it on your calendar to make the appointment. Ask questions, make sure you understand your condition, takes notes, if necessary, and then follow your doctor's recommendations. Remember that you are responsible for your health, no one else.

Exercise: Joining a health club or senior center and working out three to five times a week is great for those who can afford it and want club benefits. But if you discover, after searching your own personality and preferences very carefully that you will not go somewhere else to exercise, establish your own ritual at home. You can buy all kinds of exercise equipment, or just buy three to five pound dumbbells, an exercise CD, or a book, and create your own program.

Walking is probably the best exercise of all. If you don't like walking alone, team with a friend, or get a dog, A dog will make you walk no matter what, and will provide a companion to talk to and sing to. "Sing?" You may be thinking. "Does anyone sing to a dog?" I do. I sing to my fluffy, white

Maltese, Bailey. And he wags his tail in appreciation every time. Or maybe it isn't appreciation; maybe it's because I am paying attention to him.

The benefits of having a dog are many, including exercise, companionship, and love. There are, however, drawbacks, so you should think carefully before rushing out to obtain a dog (or a cat, for that matter). Below are a few matters to consider:

—Would I want a special breed of dog? Must the dog have purebred registrations? Or would I be happy with a dog from a local animal shelter?

Purebred dogs often cost hundreds of dollars, while the payment for shelter dogs is relatively minimal depending on the community and its regulations. Often, shelter dogs have to be neutered upon or before adoption, and unless a dog is to be bred, it is a good idea to neuter purebred dogs also.

—Is my home "dog friendly"?

A houseful of priceless antiques may not be the best place for a big, black Labrador with a strong wagging tail. Think about where a dog would sleep, whether you have a yard or other area where a dog may enjoy the outdoors without a leash, and whether you have an appropriate place for a "doggie door".

—Can I afford to take care of a dog?

Let's face it. Urban dogs cost. Maybe not as much as a child, but, depending on how generous you want to be, close. Below are some of the necessities:

| | |
|---|---|
| — Dog food and treats | — Bed or crate |
| — Dog water and food bowl s | — Dog shampoo, toothpaste and brush |
| — leash | — Place to wash a dog |
| — Coat (in cold climates) | — Balls and other toys |
| — Immunizations | — Checkups by a veterinary |
| — License (in some areas) | |

Whether you choose a dog that sheds or does not shed, there is a downside. If a dog sheds, you will have the chore of constantly cleaning and vacuuming dog hair. If a dog does not shed, it must be "groomed", that is, have a haircut, from time to time: generally every one to three months.

If you decide to have your dog trained by a professional trainer, this would be another expense.

—Who would take care of my dog while I am away?

My daughter gave Bailey to me for an early Christmas present. When she asked that I pick a dog from pictures supplied by the breeder, the puppies were so cute I couldn't resist the present, but only with the provision that my daughter take care of the dog if I wanted to travel. She has, but I realize not everyone has such a responsible family member. Of course, you can leave your dog in a kennel or take it with you, although either option can be expensive. Consider carefully what you would do.

Diet. In the chapter on food, I will discuss more about diet, but suffice it to say that the amount and type of food you eat daily and the amount that you weigh may make a big difference in how you think of yourself and your entire view of life.

Housekeeping: If you have not previously been in charge of it, maintenance of your home and other matters of daily living can be daunting. Generally, men have a harder time with household chores and cooking, while women are more likely to be intimidated with the care of vehicles, home maintenance, and the yard. While we may have helped with part of these tasks, if we were not in charge of scheduling and seeing that a task or project is completed, we may not have a clue about how to make it happen smoothly. If you already know how to maintain a home and the other necessities of life, you may be tempted to skip this part, but don't. There may be some things you can do better or some things you can discard.

The following are some suggestions to make your single life easier and more organized. The first rule is to put things back in their place after you use them. In other words, to quote a friend, "don't put it down, put it away".

Second, review your finances, make calls to a few cleaning services, and determine if you can afford to have someone clean your home once a month or every two weeks. If you can, and don't mind having someone else cleaning your home, hire a housekeeper. You will be surprised at how good you feel when you know that the dust, grime and dirt are gone or will be gone shortly.

If you cannot reasonably afford help, you will have to do the cleaning yourself. If your health does not permit this, enlist the aid of your family or friends. Don't despair. And, unless you are determined or have to, because you are working or volunteering, to get your housework completed all at once, you can spread out cleaning chores over the week, an hour or so each day. Do clean at least every other week, a chore that is easier if you pick up and touch up a few minutes every day. Don't, on the other hand, make cleaning an obsession, the whole meaning of your life. It's not.

Fortunately, with our modern conveniences, laundry can be done any time while you are reading, watching TV or playing with the dog. Sort clothes into piles by color and fabric and plop them into the washing machine, then into the dryer. Just make sure you are there to take clothes out of the dryer to hang them up right away. To make your clothes cleaning easier, read labels when shopping to make sure that a garment is washable. If not, don't buy it, or create a separate space for clothes that need to go to the dry cleaners. Some articles may have to be ironed. If you don't know how, ask your daughter, your spouse's best friend, or a neighbor. Or, if you can't picture yourself ironing, take those clothes to a laundry.

In addition to walking or exercising, plan an activity every day that will get you out of the house. This can be doing yard work, playing golf or tennis, shopping, having lunch or dinner with a friend (or by yourself), attending a club meeting, playing cards, going to a movie or play, attending church, getting your hair cut or your nails done; that is, any activity you can look forward to. If the weather is bad, you can cancel or reschedule.

<u>Driving:</u> Unless you are physically or mentally unable to drive safely, keep driving. Drive yourself wherever you want to go, drive others, drive during the day, drive at night. Sometimes, as we get older, we hesitate or refuse to

go out at night, often using the excuse that we don't see well. Don't give in to this fun-limiting attitude. Of course, if a doctor confirms you cannot drive in the dark, you shouldn't. But there are so many aids today to assist with glare and with directions, your timidity should not be an excuse to keep you from getting out, no matter what the time of day.

Chances are, if you and your spouse were both drivers, you now have two or more vehicles. Consider selling the oldest car or the one with the most mileage. Or, if your finances allow, sell or trade both cars to buy a new gas efficient model.

Keeping your car in good condition is important. Keep the gas tank full, have regular oil changes and tune-ups, wash the car inside and out, and buy new tires as needed. If you know nothing about cars, read the manual, and discuss maintenance and care with your family or friends. If your car is old and not in good running order, consider buying a new or newer model used one. The important consideration in today's world is to avoid having your car break down, or run out of gas when you are alone. If you do have car trouble or run out of gas, pull over as safely as possible to the side of the road and stop the motor, but don't get out. Use your cell phone (which should always be with you) to call your emergency service provider, such as AAA; then wait in the car for them to arrive. Never get into a car with someone you don't know!

There are a few important things you should keep in your trunk. You should have a blanket, if you live in a cold climate, a box of crackers, a couple of bottles of water, a flashlight, a snow scraper, and canvas bags with handles for groceries. You should also consider jumper cables and a shovel. Be sure to change perishables periodically.

If you don't know how to drive a car, or can't drive because of your age or infirmities, you will have to rely on public transportation or friends. Almost all large cities and suburbs, even mid-sized communities, have a variety of transportation choices like light rail, buses, taxis, and senior services. Many local transportation companies, senior centers, community centers, and retirement communities offer group transportation to grocery stores and shopping centers, as well as individual trips to doctors and other destinations. These services often require a fee and scheduling ahead. Check with your local government and senior centers to see what is available to you. If no public transportation is available, you will have to rely on family and friends.

Write lists. Lists of groceries needed. Lists of projects. Lists of goals. A day-timer, calendar, or electronic device is useful to record appointments, activities and important things to do on any given day. Review the lists and calendar every day; update or delete items as necessary. It is surprising (or maybe not) how keeping lists and writing down goals and aspirations, makes a person not only more productive, but more interested in life and interesting to others.

Pick out one or two needs or wants you have thought about, write them in big letters at the top of a blank sheet and then itemize what has to be done to accomplish these goals. Put the list on your refrigerator or your desk and mark off the steps as you accomplish them. You will not only soon achieve your goals, but will feel satisfied and proud of the fact that you did so. By focusing on and planning events you want to happen, you will be more optimistic and less likely to dwell on the past.

Find Joy: Most people, when asked if they are happy, may find it difficult to answer. In my experience, the word " happy" conjures up a mental image of a person who, with not a care in the world, dances around to some ethereal music, all the while smiling and laughing as colorful butterflies and rose petals fall from the sky. Most of us, if not all of us, realize that if we were in this merry state of mind constantly, both we and other people would think we were crazy. Consequently, some people will flatly say "no". Others will qualify their answer with something like "part of the time" or "generally" or "it depends on what you mean by happy".

The upbeat people I know are not deliriously "happy" but rather are contented, with moments of sorrow, moments of anger, problems to solve, people to love, dreams of the future, and many moments of joy. And those moments of joy are the key to feeling good about your life.

Find joy every day. Find it in the laughter of a baby or friend; find it discovering the first flower of spring, even if it is a bright yellow dandelion.

Find joy in a beautiful sunset; in that unlikely delicious concoction you made for dinner; in accomplishing a goal; in buying an addition to your antique collection for a dollar at a garage sale; in cleaning out your closet. Joy is when you finally get that grumpy old man who comes in your office every day to smile; when you secure a new order, when you finish filling out your tax return; when you catch a fish. There is joy when you give a compliment or gift to another, and likewise, when you receive one. The point I am trying to make is, solve problems, limit anger and sorrow, and find many bits of joy every day. And, when you go to bed, dwell on remembering your bits of joy, instead of problems or troubles. You can do little about problems after you go to bed, but worrying about them will keep you awake. Counting your blessings will help you sleep better.

Learn to Play: Do you remember when you were a child being so absorbed in some activity that you didn't want to quit for any reason, even to eat? "Just one more lap around the pool," you would say to your mom. Or "I'll be there as soon as I finish coloring this page." Or "Let me just finish this chapter of my book." Or "I'll be there in a minute, but we need to finish this game."

There are three points the above statements by children illustrate. The first point is that they are doing something absorbing and fun—activities they love and want to continue and which often have no requirement for a goal or accomplishment. In other words, they want to play. You will notice, however, that each of their statements includes a goal of some kind. This brings me to the second point. We are taught from an early age that activities of whatever kind must have a goal. So, in order to satisfy an adult's requirement for accomplishment, these children have learned to include a goal in their replies to the pleas to end their activity, instead of merely admitting they want to go on with their play. Mere play without a goal, they have been taught, is frivolous.

I maintain playing is *not* a waste of time if we understand that doing something we love; something absorbing, relaxing and fun, is worthwhile even if the endeavor, in a real sense, accomplishes nothing other than a feeling of well-being. The main thing is to make time in your life to do things you love even if the activity may be described by others as silly.

The third point to remember is that everyone defines play as something different. What one person may define as work may be play to another person. Your play may be to dance or sing or play baseball. Another's play may be to read or write a novel, a family history, or short stories. Some people can only relax if they are entertained by others, so they spend time watching television, or attending plays, or going to the movies. My neighbor plays golf several times a week. My aunt smiles when she is knitting. My friend Mildred loves tending to her garden and sharing the vegetables she grows there. The clue is to think about what you have thoroughly enjoyed in the past, what engenders your passion, what activity absorbs you so much that you forget the time or other obligations. Then, make time in your life to play and discard those guilt feelings for accomplishing nothing other than enjoyment.

Men, in my experience, find it easier to find time for play. Think about it! No weekend chore, like mowing the lawn, or repairing a squeaky stair step, or changing the oil in the car, will deter a man from his golf game, or going fishing with the next door neighbor. On the other hand, a woman will feel she has to do the shopping, or water the plants, or dust the living room, or a myriad of other, often not urgent duties, before or instead of giving herself permission to do something playful. One woman I know consistently canceled playing cards with her friends, and when I asked if she did this because she didn't like playing cards, she frowned and thought for a moment. "Actually," she said, "I love to play cards and visit with my friends. When we are playing and talking, I don't think about what I should be doing, but as soon as it's over, I start thinking about what I could have accomplished if I had stayed home. Besides," she added, "my husband plays golf and goes fishing on Wednesdays and Fridays, so I think I should be with him on the days he is home."

What's wrong with her picture? Obviously, she had not given herself permission to enjoy playing from time to time, nor had she realized that duties and keeping her company never interfered with her husband's play time. He knew how to play and relax without feeling guilty about missed obligations and her company, but she needs to learn to indulge in activities that give her pleasure and don't necessarily accomplish anything tangible without feeling guilty.

Keeping busy is the best way to avoid loneliness; however, busyness does not always have to be taking care of the necessities of life, earning a living, or accomplishing your goals. Busyness should include the activities that you love and make you happy. Think back to your childhood and young adulthood and remember the pursuits during those years that made you happy. Was it dancing? Fishing? Hiking? Reading? Rollerblading? Skiing? When in your heart of hearts you find satisfying, joyful interests of old, incorporate those feasible activities into your life now, or find new pleasure and ways to play. Life, again, will become interesting.

**Treasure the past, embrace the future**

# MOVING

There are many reasons why you may consider moving. Do your age and infirmities prevent you from caring for yourself and your current home? Is your home too large for one person? Do you dislike your home or the neighborhood? Would you like to be closer to family or friends? Is your home too expensive for your new income level? Can you mow, trim, plant and otherwise maintain a large yard? Can you think of any other reason why you think you should change your habitat? Give this some thought.

Sometimes an adult child, or another relative, usually with good intentions, will insist on sharing either the parent's or the relative's home. This can be a good solution if either the parent or a child is having financial difficulty maintaining a home alone. It can also be a disaster.

When Emma's husband died, her divorced daughter insisted that her mother move in with her. Since Emma didn't work and was generally home, the arrangement worked well because it not only allowed the two to share expenses, but solved the day care problem for the daughter who had a small child. When the daughter remarried, she informed her new husband that she came as part of a package and expected her mother as well as her child to live with them. He agreed. They bought a house that had two master bedrooms, so Emma had her own room and bathroom. Emma lived with them for thirty years until her death.

Margaret's experience with living in her son's home was quite different. There was apparently friction between Margaret and her daughter-in-law from the moment Margaret moved in. First, Margaret didn't like living in the basement, even though she had her own room and bath. She didn't like the stairs or the dampness. She was a dedicated homemaker who liked everything neat and clean, but her daughter-in-law hated housekeeping. Neither liked to cook, but when they did, they criticized each other's cooking. Margaret did not have a car, so she was dependent on her son and his wife to take her anywhere; a chore they came to resent. In short, the atmosphere in the home became so tense that after two years, Margaret found a room in a small, inexpensive retirement home which offered transportation for outings and meals and moved without even notifying her son that she was going. They haven't spoken to each other since. A very sad experience, which I think might have been avoided if Margaret and her son had given some realistic thought to his and her needs and expectations.

The point of these two experiences is that before you move in with another family or allow them to reside in your home, consider carefully your relationship with them, your way of life, your values, and your expectations and compare these elements with theirs.

Unless you cannot maintain your current home because of your age or health, in which case you should consider some sort of assisted living arrangement, don't move for at least a year. A year will give you time to decide how and where you want to live, to sort through your belongings, to explore all of your options and, hopefully, to find the right solution to your needs. And you may find that, after some adjustments, the place where you currently live suits you just fine, especially if you already live in a condominium or townhouse.

If, at the end of a year, you decide to change your residence, consider the ideal lifestyle you would like to have. Consider what your finances allow, and whether or not you expect overnight company from time to time. Your first thought might be that, since you are alone, a one bedroom apartment with a small kitchen and one bathroom is all you need. Being realistic, perhaps a small condominium or apartment is all you will be able to afford. Even if this is so, below are some considerations you need to think about before you decide to move. The answers to some of the questions below will require research; others will be based upon your likes, dislikes and lifestyle. You may want to jot down the answers for further contemplation and reference.

1. How much money can you reasonably expect from the sale of your current home, or, if renting, what is your current rent? A realtor can help you with this by comparing sales of similar homes in your area with yours.

2. What are you able or willing to pay for a new home or rental?

3. Where would you like to live? In the same neighborhood? In another part of your town or city? In another state or town? In a retirement community that offers social and recreational amenities and meals?

4. How many bedrooms and bathrooms would you like to have? The answer to this will depend on whether you expect to have overnight visitors, although it is often possible to rent a nearby motel room for occasional visitors to provide them with a bathroom of their own and privacy.

5. Do you want a garage? Does it matter if the garage is attached, or merely close by?

6. Are you willing to take care of a yard and outside maintenance?

7. Do you need air conditioning?

8. How close to shopping and health care would you like to be?

9. How much closet and storage space do you need?

10. Do you want a den, or other space for a computer or desk?

11. Would you like to have a pantry?

12. Would you like space for a washer and dryer? Where?

13. Do you want a basement?

14. How many cabinets and drawers do you need in a kitchen for your pot, pans, dishes, and foodstuffs? This will require an inventory of your current kitchen. What will you discard and what will you take?

15. What furniture do you want to keep? What furnishings are expendable? What new furnishings would you like to or be willing to buy?

16. What else can you think of about a new home that is important to you?

When you are shopping for a new home, take your list with you to remind yourself periodically what items are necessary and what are merely nice to have.

Chances are, if you do decide to move, it will be to a smaller place because you do not need as much room. And since most of us are not willing or cannot afford to give away all the furniture and furnishings we already have, it is a good idea to assess your current belongings before you start looking for another place to live. Identify the furniture you definitely want to keep, the possibilities, and finally, the rejects to be given away or discarded. Measure the keepers and the possibilities. Keep the list in your pocket or purse along with a measuring tape, so when you are looking at new places to live, you can measure the rooms and make sure your "must have" furniture will fit.

Before moving far from your current family and friends, carefully examine your reasons for doing so. It is tempting to want to move to Florida or Arizona, or some other enticing place, but keep in mind that it is often more difficult for a single person to make friends in a totally new area. Additionally, the hot summer weather, extra bugs, humidity, and lack of seasons may not be worth milder winters. If your only complaint is shoveling snow, consider living in a community where a home owner's association takes care of ice, snow, mowing, and outside maintenance; then, if you can afford it, arrange vacations in the south during the worst of the winter, and vacations during the hot part of the summer in the mountains.

Okay. Let's assume you find the perfect place and know the date when it will be yours. If you are buying your new home, generally, a certified inspector will have made sure that appliances are in good working order and that there are no structural problems. On your part, it is a good idea to complete remodeling, painting, replacing carpets and floors, and building of shelves before you move. If you decide to rent, make sure that the air conditioner, furnace, and other appliances are in good working order.

Often, a landlord will paint before you move in and may even replace carpeting and other flooring, but, if you wish to change anything yourself, you will have to obtain the landlord's permission.

Your new home will be satisfying to you if you pick colors you like and can live with for a long period of time. Go to a paint store where they have little cards of paint colors, pick out the ones you like, and then choose paint, carpet and fabric in those colors. Be careful not to let decorators or friends or family talk you into colors they like. Insist on yours. Remember that generally neutral or "cool" colors tend to make a room look bigger, and dark walls tend to shrink a room. If you love dark or bright warm colors, try using them as accents, by painting only one wall of a room, and/or placing assorted accessories. Paint can always be changed, but, since we tend to keep fabrics and furniture for long times, even years, these should be chosen carefully to reflect the taste and style which make you most comfortable.

When it comes time to pack, since you have already decided what to take and what to give away and where furniture and furnishings will be placed, the move should go smoothly. Enlist the aid of family, friends or movers, but supervise the packing closely and do your own labeling of boxes so that you know what is in each and where that box or furniture should be placed. When your household goods arrive at the new place, again, closely supervise and/or unpack yourself so that articles are where you want them and can be found easily.

As soon as possible, put away and arrange your belongings and furniture the way you want. To give yourself some urgency and a deadline, consider giving a party about two weeks after your move. The party doesn't have to involve a large number of people, or elaborate refreshments, but the prospect of showing off your new home in the best light possible will inspire you to organize your household much faster than if you are the only one who sees it.

**Where my home will be is up to me**

# PREPARING TO COOK

Frequently I am asked, "How do you cook for one?" The question is asked not only by individuals who have recently lost their partners, but also, surprisingly, I think, by people who have lived alone for several years. Before answering the question, I ask "How did you know how much to cook for two? Or for more, when your children were still at home?" The answer to my question is generally. "Well, I bought just enough for two." Or, "When my children were still living at home, I doubled a recipe, or at least made sure there was enough for everyone."

My answer to the question of how to cook for one, then, is "Use the same principal you used to cook for two or more. Instead of adjusting buying and cooking to feed several people, adjust your buying and cooking to feed only one. Most recipes can be halved or quartered as well as doubled."

When you are first left alone, the temptation will be great to load up on frozen dinners and granola bars. Before you dump everything out of the refrigerator and freezer and rush off to the grocery store for boxes of frozen meals, think carefully. Do you like TV dinners or are they just easy? Do you know how to cook? If yes, and you like it, plan to keep doing it. If you don't know how to cook, but love good food, now is the time to experiment. Good cooking is not only pleasing for the stomach, but it is a way to satisfy a creative nature. Men, who often have little experience, maybe only barbecuing from time to time, frequently find cooking challenging and fun. And with their logical, yet creative, minds, they can be very good at it. So, men, try it. If, after cooking your own meals for a month or two, you decide you absolutely hate planning meals and cooking, I have suggestions both for eating well with a minimum of "scratch" cooking and for satisfying your hunger with no cooking at all. Whatever you decide in the long run, at least try the following preparations.

Whether you have prepared meals all your life or are just starting, a comprehensive cook book is essential. Pick a book that includes all types of meat, poultry and fish with discussions of use and care of various foods, calorie counts, and hints for cooking as well as recipes. This overall cook book will be large and need not necessarily contain gourmet cooking which can be found in smaller targeted books. Personally, I like and use The New Doubleday Cookbook by Jean Anderson which, though published in 1990, can still be found in bookstores or on the internet at a discount.

If your spouse had cookbooks, keep them all for now, but realize as you experiment, they can be discarded or given away later. Also, now is the time to go through old recipes, whether they are on your computer or on cards in a box. Toss out or give away those concoctions you have not or will not make, being careful to preserve those you love.

Earlier, you were cautioned not to get rid of your extra freezer. If you don't have a freezer in addition to the one with your refrigerator, buy one. The least expensive one, even a small one, will do. When you are cooking for one, you need plenty of freezer space to keep portioned meals.

You may think shopping at warehouse grocery stores such as Sam's Club or Costco is crazy for a single person since their packaging is monstrous. Not so. If you don't already have a membership, sign up right away. No matter whether you have plenty of money or not, there is no use spending more than you have to for the necessities of life. All that is required is planning, repackaging and storage.

Time to go shopping. Here is the key. I try not to go shopping when I am hungry. I go right after lunch, or breakfast, or dinner, to avoid buying food that I don't need or that is full of unnecessary calories.

I buy paper towels, toilet paper, napkins, garbage bags, plastic freezer bags, plastic wrap, foil, laundry and dishwasher soap etc. in the large quantities offered by the discount store. When I arrive home, I store these items on shelves in my garage, basement, or a large closet. The money and time I save by buying in large quantities is worth the small extra effort.

Meat, fish, nuts, dried cranberries, coffee, cereal, dried pasta, refrigerated tortellini or ravioli—anything that can be frozen, or doesn't have to be refrigerated—I purchase in large warehouse quantities, including orange juice (not from concentrate) and milk in gallon containers. O.J. usually has a "use date" far enough in the future that I know I will use it before then.

Milk can be poured into pint or quart plastic containers and frozen. Caution! Don't fill the container too full; liquid, when frozen, expands. The milk will look weird in the freezer because the butterfat clings to the sides of the container, but if you take it out of the freezer and put it into the refrigerator a day or two before you want to use it, it will thaw into good looking milk again. Shake it and use it.

You can buy large bags of frozen vegetables and fruits, like peas, corn and broccoli, as long as they are loose so you can grab a handful and cook for any meal. Don't buy fresh vegetables in large quantities; you probably can't eat them before they spoil. Do buy berries and nuts in season and freeze them. If you don't wash the berries before putting them in the freezer, they will freeze separately so you can use any small quantity just by spraying them with cool water.

Bread can be frozen, though personally, I am not a fan of doing it, because the texture is not the same as fresh bread. Experiment and decide for yourself. Muffins and particularly English muffins, wrapped separately, taste fine after being frozen. Likewise, cookies and cakes, if wrapped separately, may take care of your sweet tooth. A word of caution, however; if you have overweight issues or dietary problems, don't buy ice cream or cookies or chips or any other food you shouldn't have. If you don't have them in your home, you won't be tempted to eat them.

My regular grocery store is where I buy all the rest of my food because I can buy in small quantities, or large quantities on sale to be apportioned at home. I choose small cans of vegetables and fruits and the smallest jars of condiments such as salad dressing, mayonnaise, and ketchup. I select small quantities of fresh vegetables and fruit, being careful to buy only what you can reasonably eat in a few days.

Do not be afraid to put a small quantity of foods such as cherries, grapes, or bananas, anything that is sold by the pound, in a separate bag.

You don't have to buy the whole amount put together by the grocery store. And just because the sign says ten for a dollar, you don't have to buy ten. The store should charge you at the discounted rate only for what you take. If the store resists, go elsewhere.

When you arrive home with your groceries, here is what you do. This will take a few minutes, but will save you time in the long run.

— Take meats and fish out of their packaging, unless they are already packaged individually. Wrap steaks, chops, fish and hamburger in individual portions in plastic wrap; then place as many of the items as possible in a large plastic freezer bag. Double wrapping frozen items in plastic reduces the risk of freezer burn.

— Cut as many ribs as you can eat at one meal, wrap and freeze.

— Buy hamburger in patties, wrap each patty separately so you can use one or as many as you need. If your grocer does not offer the convenience of patties, you will have to make them yourself.

— Wrap muffins, English muffins, and slices of bread individually in plastic, then put into a freezer bag.

— Cut cakes into one serving slices, wrap and freeze.

— Place one serving of cookies into a plastic bag and freeze.

— Put fresh berries and nuts in plastic containers without washing them, and freezeTake out and wash only what you want to use for one meal.

— Remove ravioli and tortellini from the refrigerator package, repackage in individual servings, put in a plastic freezer bag, and freeze.

— Label each freezer bag with the name of the food, date it, add cooking instructions, and throw the bag in the freezer. You can now use the amount you need, whether for one or five, and the rest will not spoil.

— Try to use the oldest foods in you freezer first.

If you are moaning that you will have to give up roasts, don't despair. Go ahead and buy ham, pork, beef, or a roasting chicken, roast it, eat what you want for one meal, and then cut the rest into individual portions and freeze as above. If you make gravy, this can be frozen too. Likewise, if you make a big pot of spaghetti sauce or chili or stew, divide into portions sufficient for one meal and freeze in containers. All of these may be taken out when you want them and micro waved for instant home cooked meals. And, if you have company, you can take out one or two or three more portions.

On the door of the freezer, use a magnet or two to attach a list written in pencil of what is on each freezer shelf. When you use foods, erase that food from your list, or add new foods. You will know at a glance what you have in the freezer, what shelf it is on, and how many portions you have.

Fresh vegetables cannot all be treated the same. Generally, root vegetables like potatoes, carrots, turnips, onions, and beets (not the tops) will last in your refrigerator crisper for a month or longer, if they are not stored in plastic bags. These vegetables also keep well stored at room temperature, ideally in a cool, dark place. Garlic should be kept in a jar that has holes to allow air to circulate.

Buy small quantities of tomatoes (the ones with the stems keep the longest), only one or two summer squash, zucchini, ears of corn, green onions, broccoli and sweet peppers, and eat them within a few days. Note that if you use green or red peppers in cooking, you can cut out the cores, quarter them, and without washing, put them into a freezer bag and freeze. Then just take out the amounts you need, wash them, cut up, and use.

Lettuce, asparagus and celery need special care to keep one or two weeks. Don't buy head (iceberg) lettuce unless you plan to use it in less than a week. Instead, buy leaf or romaine lettuce. Probably when you buy lettuce or celery at the store, you will have placed them in a plastic bag. When you get home, keep these in the bag, situating the cut end into a bottom corner of the bag, sprinkle water on the top, and prop the lettuce or celery up as much as you can in the crisper so that the water falls into the corner with the cut end. Remind yourself that these were once growing plants and just as flowers will last after you cut them if you place them in water, so will these plants. Asparagus, similarly, will last longer if you put the stems, cut side down, in a container of water in the refrigerator. Fresh herbs like basil, parsley, cilantro and dill will also keep well if placed, cut stem down, in water and refrigerated.

The longevity of fruits varies. Bananas need to be eaten in two or three days, so break up the quantities offered in the grocery store. Buy no more than three, at least two still green, if you can. Apples will last two to five weeks; grapes and cherries for a week or so; peaches and pears for a week; oranges for two or three weeks, all in the refrigerator. Avocados need not be refrigerated, if used in a day or two, but may be kept cold for several days and then taken out to ripen. You may have to experiment to determine the right amount of time for refrigeration and ripening.

**Advance preparation**
**Minimizes cooking frustration.**

# COOKING AND EATING

Okay, you have food bought in small portions or frozen in single servings. Now what? How do you cook it for one?

I am not going to tell you what to cook or how to cook it. That is the duty of your cookbooks and your own likes and dislikes. If you have cooked all your life, having read that this is not a recipe book, you may be tempted to skip this chapter. Please don't. Cooking for one takes not only the same planning as cooking for more people, but also a good deal more math, and plenty of trial and error.

The first thing to do is to take out or look up the recipes of foods you like the most. If the recipe is for four, divide the ingredients into quarters or thirds, depending upon your appetite and whether you want to have leftovers for another meal. If for six, divide by six. You get the picture. This method works for anything that doesn't have to rise, like cakes or cookies, since changing the ingredients in baked goods doesn't necessarily mean less baking soda or powder. If you make these desserts, follow the recipe, then either cut into portions and freeze, or give some to the neighbors.

Since most people know how to make a sandwich and pour cereal into a bowl, I'm not going to waste time telling you how to prepare lunches or breakfasts. Suffice it to say that I strive to include all the basic food groups in my everyday eating. A healthy diet is important; however, almost without exception, the people I interviewed for this book said it makes life more interesting if they allowed themselves to have bacon and eggs, fast food lunches, or other food splurges once in a while.

So on to the main meal of the day; that is, dinner. Once again, I'm not going to tell you what to cook or when to eat it. Some people eat a big meal at noon, some at eight in the evening. Suit yourself, though you should try to eat around the same time each day whenever possible. In any case, try not to eat a heavy meal later than eight in the evening or you will pay with weight gain and restless, uncomfortable sleep. The key to good health and good appetite is variety of food and making your meals pretty. Yes, pretty! Think of what your meals look like in good restaurants. Each plate is arranged artfully with meat, a colorful vegetable, potato or pasta, and often a sprig of parsley. Consider doing the same. When you do, you cannot help but create a meal that is not only appetizing, but healthy.

If you have prepared meals before, you know that one of the hardest tasks is to have everything ready at the same time. Consider timing of each item before you start cooking. A roast can take hours, vegetables a few minutes. Avoid doing what a friend of mine, an inexperienced cook, did at his first dinner party. He started everything at once, and when he judged (not always rightly) that an item was cooked, we ate it; then waited for the next item. The meal took hours. A memorable experience, but not one to repeat.

Let's start with salad. Since you are cooking for one, no need to make a big bowl of salad. Just take out a salad plate, tear up some lettuce, and cover the plate. Then add small cut up portions of fresh vegetables such as, but not limited to, carrots, onions, tomatoes, peppers, celery or an avocado. Then, for variety and color, add a small handful of dried cranberries, or nuts, and, on top, a sprinkle of shredded cheese. Beautiful and appetizing. Sometimes, I even throw on a few frozen blueberries, or grapes. Add your favorite salad dressing and you have a salad fit for a queen or a king.

Next, your entree. Start with simple recipes, and as you become comfortable or excited about cooking, try the more complicated. Eventually, you may even want to buy gourmet cookbooks. Since you have frozen meat or fish in one serving size packets, cook them, using your favorite divided recipe. Or, if you cook a roast, eat what you want that day or maybe the next, then cut up the rest into single servings and freeze for easy meals later. If you like grilled meat and fish, using your outdoor barbecue, though tasty, can be time consuming and not always available, particularly if you live in a area where it snows. Consequently, consider buying a medium-sized indoor grill; one that can be used for one or two people, or more. You may have guests from time to time. Make your entree appealing and healthy by adding a cooked vegetable and a starch such as potatoes, pasta or beans.

Vegetables are generally easy. Use a small microwavable dish with a lid, add a small amount of water and the vegetable, including but not limited to, green beans, yellow squash, broccoli, red potatoes, zucchini, beets, and cabbage, and microwave for three to five minutes, depending on how you like a particular vegetable cooked. Pour off the water; then, if you wish, add your favorite topping like cheese or butter, turn on again for 20 seconds and you have a quickly and perfectly cooked side dish.

Desserts are optional, but if you must have one, try to keep portions small. If your weight says you shouldn't eat desserts or snacks, don't make or buy them. On the other hand, if you like a cocktail or glass of wine before dinner, have one . . . emphasis on one . . . with maybe a little dividend. Any more and you may forget to eat that fabulous meal you prepared all on your own.

Okay. You are ready to eat. Two suggestions to keep in mind. First, always set the table or TV tray with at least a place mat, utensils, condiments and napkin. This presentation together with your "pretty" entree and salad will help you to eat slower and with dignity, instead of wolfing your food down all at once. Second, contrary to pundits who say you should not eat in front of the TV, I encourage you as a single person to do so. If I watch the news or a program I enjoy, I do not feel lonely or miss dinner conversation with someone else. There is nothing lonelier than eating at a table alone with no one to talk to or no one to see.

After a month or so of cooking your meals from scratch, you will know whether you like to cook, or just want to eat. One alternative is to eat a big meal at a restaurant every day like my neighbor, Phil. His solution to keeping the cost reasonable is to eat breakfast and an evening snack at home, then to eat his main meal out. He frequently takes advantage of "early bird" dinners, or the reduced cost of a late lunch at inexpensive restaurants.

If you eat out frequently, you may often go alone. Men generally have no problem eating out alone, but some women are reluctant to do so. If you find yourself reluctant to be seen in public without another person, now is the time to push the sides of your comfort box. Believe me, no one is looking at you, no other diners care that you sit by yourself, and the bonus is that the waiters will pay more attention to you. Good waiters may even get to know you and what you like to eat if you go to the same place frequently enough.

The middle ground of the two extremes above is a mixture. Stock one or two frozen dinners, try one of the new prepared refrigerated entrees, and prepare meals from a box. Eat out sometimes for a treat, bring home fast food when you are tired, try the new dinner businesses available in some cities that allow you to pick entrees with various sides to take home, and cook those recipes you love. Don't hesitate to try new gourmet concoctions when you feel like something special. In any case, stock your freezer and refrigerator as noted above, taking into consideration that you will not be cooking every dinner.

**Cooking for one can be satisfying and fun.**

# FAMILY AND FRIENDS

"Sometimes," Mae said during our interview, "I really have to push myself to get ready to go somewhere, but as soon as I am out of the house, I am glad I made the effort. I really enjoy being with friends or my family or even shopping. On the other hand," she laughed, "I'm like a kid. I love snow days when I have an excuse to stay home and read."

When you live alone, you need support, conversation and contact with other people. Good friends and frequent communication with your family are necessary to ward off being lonely; however, don't forget to devote time to endeavors that you can do by yourself.

Family: It is important to stay in close contact with your family. Call your children frequently, no less than once a month or more often. With the current telephone plans available, long distance within the U.S. is generally free, so call far away family whenever you can.

If your children, or grandchildren or other relatives live reasonably close to you, here are some suggestions to spend time with them:

— Plan activities with your children. Do lunch at least once a month with one or more of them. If appropriate, take them to a play or concert or a ball game. Have a barbecue.

— Take your grandchildren to a movie, or to an amusement park, or a museum, or out for a pizza. Invite them for a "sleep-over" at your house.

— Offer to plan or assist your children or other relatives with birthday parties and Christmas and Thanksgiving and the Fourth of July.

Be careful not to overwhelm your family with your presence all of the time; they undoubtedly have friends and activities which need not be part of your life; but do let them know that they are important to you. In other words, share special occasions with your family, but don't expect your children for every Sunday chicken dinner or any other weekly activity like grocery shopping, mowing your lawn, shoveling snow, or taking out the garbage, unless you are physically unable to do these chores. Taking care of household needs yourself keeps you busy, independent and interested in your surroundings.

Here is where your positive thoughts need to rule! If someone forgets your birthday, or to say thank you for a gift, or doesn't invite you to a party, or something similar, don't be mad. It doesn't mean you are not loved or that the gift wasn't appreciated, or that they don't like your company; it just means they forgot or that the party was just for their friends. Shrug off the incident and forget it. Similarly, offer to help family members in a way that you can without being insistent. Be concerned and sympathetic when they have setbacks or trouble, but never criticize. And don't pry into their affairs or way of living; they won't appreciate your nosiness any more than you would if they pried into yours. Even though it may be hard at times, always keep your interaction with your children loving, encouraging, and cordial.

Whether you have children or not, remember that family includes brothers and sisters, nieces and nephews and cousins. And, if you have had issues with family members in the past which prevented you from contact with them, mend your fences. Swallow your pride, reach out to that child or sibling, and create a new relationship. No family feud is worth the loss of contribution and caring a family member can add to your life.

Friends: Association with friends, both those that you already have, and new ones, if you don't already know it, is what will keep your life interesting. The week after your loss, you should call, e-mail, or write to your friends, both those that are single and couples, to tell them how much you appreciate their help or their friendship. Then, as time passes, stay in contact with them to let them know you still want them as friends.

A common complaint I hear of the newly singled is that there is no one to talk to; that is, no one with whom to share the day's events, thoughts about the current status of their life and the world, and to help make decisions. Find a friend, preferably, but not necessarily, someone who has similar circumstances to yours, a widow or widower with common interests and financial status to yours. Call and get together with that person frequently, share your daily experiences, your frustrations, your triumphs and your thoughts and welcome the opportunity to listen to theirs.

It is very important for single people who have no family or other support system to have caring friends. Two people I interviewed for this book have similar circumstances. Both have no family members living. Both have no children. Both live alone. Their lives, their attitudes about life, and even their health, however, are quite different.

Before Lily's husband died, she devoted her whole life to his needs, interests, business associates, and friends. In effect, she had no interests or endeavors of her own. When she found herself alone, however, she realized that because she had always been busy fulfilling her husband's desires and needs, she could not bear spending the rest of her life doing nothing just because he was gone.

"In fact" Lily said, "after moping around for a week or so, I found myself thinking about all the things I could never do when Bert was alive. I hadn't been to church in years. I've always wanted to learn to play bridge. I like to read, but never had time. And, although Bert traveled a lot, he never took me with him, or wanted to travel during his vacations. I want to see more of the world before I die."

Lily started going to church. She called the local senior center and joined a bridge group where she met two or three other ladies who became friends. After about a year, she moved into a retirement community that offered local, national and international excursions. In short, she developed a circle of friends who watched out for each other, and accomplished many of her previously unsatisfied wishes. At age seventy-eight, she is in good health and has a sparkling outlook on life.

Patricia, my neighbor, also has no family. Her one son died years ago, she was an only child, and her husband, Karl, died of cancer I hadn't seen her since Karl's funeral. When I knocked on Patricia's door and asked if she would agree to an interview, she was wearing a large faded purple dress and ragged slippers. Her hair was not combed and her face was pasty. Although later Patricia told me she had just turned age sixty, she looked much older.

I think Patricia was about to say no to my request for an interview, but after a moment she opened the door wider and let me in the house. I tried not to gasp. There were boxes and papers and junk piled on the furniture and rug in the living room, all covered with dust. She led me down a hall through a narrow lane between stacks of papers to the kitchen which was surprisingly clean. The sound from a television in the corner blared and a T.V dinner lay half eaten on the table.

"Excuse the mess," Patricia said. "I just don't seem to have the energy to clean the rest of the house. I spend almost all of my time in the kitchen reading an watching television"

"I'm sorry," I said, "I didn't mean to interrupt your dinner."

"That's okay," she said. "How could you know. Besides, I always eat when I'm hungry, not on any set schedule."

She went on to explain that she never went out and had all her groceries, mainly T.V. dinners and pizzas delivered. "I haven't seen anyone, other than the delivery people, in months" she told me. "The only people I knew before Karl died were his business associates and, of course, I don't see them anymore."

"Do you have family?" I asked gently.

"No," she replied rather wistfully. "I wish I did. My parents died when I was in my forties, I was an only child, and, since my parents' families live on The West Coast, I have had no contact with them. We were never a close family, so I don't even know their names."

She went on to admit she had made no attempt to see anyone, including a doctor or a dentist, since her husband died four years before. I went away from the interview wondering what would happen if Patricia became ill or died, and vowed to check on her periodically. A week or so later, when I saw the newspapers piling up on her porch, I called my county's Human Resource center and their representative found Patricia had been ill for several days.

The point of these two stories is that we all need a support group. We need people who care about us, people we can call and will call us, and people to have fun with. If you don't already have such a support group, it will take some effort on your part, but is certainly worth your persistence.

The following may sound strange to you, but, believe me, you need to gather up your courage and do it. Have a party. No later than three weeks after your loss, invite a few close friends or family for brunch, lunch, dinner or cocktails—whatever type of event you can manage. The party doesn't have to be elaborate. Go to the grocery store and buy snack trays, or have coffee and pastries, or a barbecue, or order a pizza. Of course, if you have been cooking all your life, make your specialty.

Ostensibly, this party is to thank family or friends for their concern during your difficult time, but the real reason is that you want them to know that you have not dropped out of their lives, that you still want to be friends, and that you have not become a recluse. Once you invite others to your home, most, but not necessarily all, will invite you back. Then, you entertain again, then they do, and so on. It is most important to invite couples as well as single people. All too often, once a person is alone, married friends drift away, particularly from women. They jump to the conclusion that women can cook and fend for themselves, while men, who often can't cook, need dinner invitations to eat right. So, when you have your party, do not try to make the guest list even. Make it clear that it is okay to have an odd number; that is, a single person with no companion, and couples. Don't forget, however, to also invite single friends to your first party or any in the future.

In order to keep your life interesting and active, try to accept every social invitation you receive. Barbecues, parties, dinner out, lunch out, theater, fishing, golf, literary club, business club, whatever. Accept an invitation even if the activity is not your favorite. You can always decline uninteresting invitations later, once you have established with family and friends that you enjoy their company and thoughtfulness for including you in their activities. Likewise, identify activities you like, and then invite a friend or friends to accompany you. Buy tickets to a play. Go bird watching. Bicycle. Ski. Go out to eat, with a friend or a group, but don't hesitate to go alone. Become involved in a least one group that meets at least once a month or more often. Devote your time to some charity. Go to church.

Support a political candidate. Attend activities at a senior center. If you live in a retirement community that offers trips and other outings, sign up and go. Buy a computer, if you don't have one, and take classes to learn how to use it. You know, or should take time to, identify your interests. Use them to get out, be interested and interesting, and to keep busy.

Renew old friendships. Have you wondered what happened to your college roommate or to the next door neighbor who moved away? To the business associate you had lunch with every day until you left to take a new job? Take time to track those past good friends down and then contact them. In most cases, old friends will love to hear from you. If so, catch up with their lives by telephone or e-mail, then invite them to visit, or for lunch or dinner, or some other fun activity. If a friend or a relative lives far away, arrange a meeting some place half-way between your homes.

Use the activities you love to develop goals, short term and long term, for living the rest of your life. Do you like to travel? Where? Do you want a better job? A different career? Your own business? To retire and play golf? To write a book? Do research. Take applicable college courses. Talk with owners of similar businesses. Start or increase you contributions to a 401(K) or other savings. Cherish the past, but don't dwell on it. Instead, always look and plan forward.

A word of caution. Try to associate with positive, uplifting people and limit your time with people who complain and criticize all the time. Attitudes of friends are catching, and you want your attitude to be optimistic and your life to be contented, even happy, not full of bitterness and anger. Your conversations with friends should be about what you and they are doing now, and what your and their plans are for the future. Reminisces of the past should be about funny things that happened, good times, and the dreams that you shared. Unless you can laugh about them, avoid talking about missed opportunities, old grudges, failures and what your life would be like if your partner were still with you. Such topics will only depress you.

When you are talking with family or friends, avoid belaboring your past experiences, a common mistake made by many older people. Most young people will be bored with accounts of how you took San Juan Hill singlehandedly, or how you had to hang sheets on a clothesline to dry in the old days, or how you walked five miles to and from school in the snow. Of course, if someone asks about something in your past, answer, but keep it brief. Don't let anyone label you as "old, boring and senile".

**People are lonely**
**Because they build walls instead of bridges.**

# GETTING AWAY

Traveling is a great way to learn about the rest of the world, to break up your routines, and take your mind off your loss. Getting away from your home forces you to plan ahead and be excited. So, if your health and finances permit, get out, go somewhere, have fun and conversations, and replenish your soul. Trips don't have to be long. They can be as simple as couple of days (never more than four, they have a life) with family or friends. Or try a few days at the beach, at a lake, or in the mountains. Longer trips, like a cruise or a tour, or, if you want to learn about the history and other data of a region, an Elderhostel program, should be taken at least once a year. Longer trips give you something to talk about with friends, both before and after, to look forward to, and to keep your thoughts about the future and not about the past.

Most of the time, especially if a trip lasts more than two days and is not in the home of a friend or relative, you will want to share it with a companion, a group of your friends, or one or more of your children or grandchildren. Consider taking some family member on a trip as a present for some special occasion, like graduation, or just for the fun of having a young excited companion.

Don't, however, rule out going by yourself. For some reason, women usually have an easier time traveling with another woman, while men are hesitant to share travel with another man. Man or woman, if you do decide to travel alone, remember rooms and cruise ship cabins will be more expensive than if you share. On the positive side, traveling alone often encourages you to make new friends and to do what you want on the trip.

The first task to travel is to decide where you want to go, how and why. Do you like warm weather, beaches and wearing summer clothes? Or would you rather go skiing or hiking in the Rocky Mountains? Would you like to bicycle through Europe? Have you always wanted to go on a cruise? Where? How long? Have you ever been to Washington, D.C? How does taking a train across Canada sound? Or would you rather trade your timeshare or rent a cabin and go fishing or hunting for a week? Remember that the planning and anticipation of a trip is at least half of the fun.

Once you decide where you want to travel, try looking at travel opportunities and reservations on the Internet. Even if you are hesitant to make arrangements yourself this way, the information will help you know what is available and approximately how much a trip will cost. If you decide not to make reservations yourself or need more help, ask around and find a good travel agent who can make suggestions and locate the best trips and prices. Ask friends and family who travel a lot to share their experiences and suggestions. By sharing your plans with others, you may find someone who wants to go with you, or who may invite you to share one of their trips. You never know unless you try.

A person who travels needs to have the paraphernalia for traveling with ease. Below are some of the things you can do to make travel convenient:

— Get rid of those old heavy suitcases. Buy light, nesting cases with wheels that are easy to store and easy to pull.
— Duplicate, to the extent sensible and necessary, makeup, shaving gear, a small hair dryer, combs, lotions, soap, a toothbrush and toothpaste, band aids, nail polish, hair spray, medications, a nail file, a small scissor, a corkscrew, and anything else you use on a daily basis to keep your self clean, comfortable, and looking good.
— Buy the smallest containers of toiletries and medications possible. If you plan to be away for a longer time than you think a small

container will last, buy two or more and throw away the item after it is empty. It may be necessary to obtain small plastic containers to fill if you can't find small prefilled products.

— Keep toiletries in see-through makeup bags or plastic bags with a zipper, or in one of those makeup travel bags that you can hang on a door handle in the bathroom. Keep these packed in your suitcase at all times. Then, each time you go somewhere, replenish the small containers from your larger at-home containers and you will be ready to go with very little fuss. No need to carry around those large, heavy shampoo bottles.

— The type, length and locality of the trip will determine what kind of clothes you should take. A rule of thumb, however, is to take clothes that can be layered and colors that can be coordinated. Limit your selection of clothes that you *will* wear not just *might* wear, take only shoes (which are heavy and take up a lot or room) which can be worn with several different outfits. In other words, pack as light as you can, and take comfortable, good looking clothes that you like, not just your new ones.

I believe taking a vacation, whether around the world or two days visiting a relative twenty miles away, is an opportunity to abandon our everyday routines, to think about something other than our daily concerns, and to renew our enthusiasm for life. I discovered not everyone views a vacation the same way.

Two friends, Jane and Susan, spent a week at Susan's timeshare in the mountains. A day or two after they returned, Susan called me.

"We had such a good time," she reported enthusiastically. "I'm sorry you were unable to go with us."

"What did you do?" I asked.

"Well, let's see. One day we went with a group on a hike to see wild flowers and a shady glade where all different kinds of mushrooms grow. The flowers were waist high and beautiful. I had no idea that there were so many colors and varieties of mushrooms. It rained two days in a row, so we read and invited two other timeshare couples for dinner and to play cards. I discovered one couple live not far from my home. I plan to invite them over for dinner and hope you will also come to meet them."

"Another day we, well, I should say, I, took the gondola to the top of a ski trail. Jane doesn't like heights, so she stayed below. The view from the top of the run was spectacular. Otherwise, we just relaxed and read and talked and took walks through the woods. It was so good to get away and to think about something different. And, of course, it was a relief to be in the mountains where it is cool."

The next day I called Jane. "You were smart not to go," she said. "The whole thing was a disaster."

"How so?" I asked, meanwhile wondering if she actually shared the same week with Susan.

"It rained half the time, for one thing, and was so cold on sunny days that I think I caught a cold. One evening, Susan invited some boring neighbors over for dinner. When we went to find something to serve them for dinner, there was only one little grocery store in that town and we had to settle for frozen chicken and canned vegetables. Awful. Another day we went on this hike to look at mushrooms, for heaven's sake. All those weeds on the way there scratched my legs and I came back covered with mosquito bites. Then Susan insisted on going up in a gondola at the ski run, so I had to wait for her with nothing do at the bottom. I just don't deal well with change and inconvenience, so was glad to get home to my normal routine."

After listening to my two friends, I decided Susan would be fun to travel with, but Jane would not. My attitude is that getting away and traveling is about a change of pace and having fun. I urge you to get out there, take all the side trips, study about the terrain and the history, explore and enjoy yourself. If you are driving, find a good local map, turn off the freeway onto byways, see little towns, visit museums and other places of interest, walk through a butterfly pavilion, laugh at the antics of groundhogs in their village, grimace at alligators, gulp as you careen down a four-wheel-drive pathway to the bottom of a mountain. Getting away from your normal life is the time to experience and enjoy all the other interesting places, people and surroundings. Let go of your staid, old inhibitions and fears and enjoy yourself, so that afterward, when you are asked, you can say enthusiastically, "I had a great time!"

**For a change of pace,**
**I will travel to another place.**

# DATING

According to U.S Census Bureau statistics of 2006, fifteen percent of the American population between ages 45 and 64 who lived alone were men; nineteen percent were women. But, because women tend to live longer than men, single men over sixty-five were only ten percent of the population, while twenty-five percent were single women. These statistics indicate that chances of finding a new companion, man or woman, are pretty good if you are under sixty-five, but men over retirement age have a decided advantage, and most women sixty-five or older will have fewer chances to date or find a companion.

Some older singles are not interested in dating. And, generally, the longer a person is single and contented, the less interested he or she is in the hassle of dating. Having said that, I hasten to add that even if you are content with living the rest of your life alone, sometimes circumstances (or match-making friends) may bring romance into your life, so be careful about making statements like "I'm not interested" or "I'll never marry again."

If you had a happy relationship with your absent partner, or if you had a bad experience with a person and yearn for a good one, the temptation will be great to search for a new mate. Be open to finding someone, but don't make the mistake of thinking that any companion would be better than being alone. If you do meet someone you like, say at work, or a reunion, or a party, or the friend of a friend, or on a cruise, or in a myriad of other places, be cautious. Don't choose a potential partner because he or she is beautiful, or powerful, or rich. Men tend to look for a woman who is younger and pretty; women want a man with money. These characteristics are not necessarily bad, but they are not the criteria you should be looking for. Instead, you need to find out if the person you are attracted to have the same values as you do, is kind and caring, likes many of the activities you like, and has a positive attitude toward life. And don't fall into the trap of a relationship with a person who needs to be rescued, saved or fixed.

A friend of mine, Marjorie, who had been a widow for about two years, began to spend time with a man who was getting a divorce because his wife had gone off with another man. "I am flattered," she told me after she had been dating James for two or three months, "because he is so attentive. He often tells me how much more understanding I am than his wife. And, I must say, we do have a good time together. It is nice to have someone to go out to dinner with and to attend parties and the theatre. The thing that bothers me is that he talks, often bitterly, about his ex-wife all the time. I know he was hurt, and I try to be sympathetic, but I wish he would focus more on our relationship."

After Marjorie and James had dated for about nine months, she confided to me, "There are some things that bother me about him. He owns a small but successful business, and when he talks about it, I realize I don't agree with some of his business practices and the way he treats his employees."

The next month, she called me and said she had broken off her relationship with James. When I inquired why she replied, "Well, for one thing, I realized James was not introducing me to his friends and family. He even whisked me away without an introduction when we ran into his son and his son's wife at a play. The final straw was when his former wife's best friend told me his wife's relationship hadn't worked out and she was returning to town."

"Did James know she was coming back?" I asked.

"Not only did he know," she replied ruefully. "When I asked him about it, he sheepishly told me that he was going to take her back; that they had been communicating for several weeks. He didn't even apologize for not telling me."

"I'm sorry," I said, thinking she must be very upset. "Don't be," she replied. "I am quite relieved. I admit I was shocked and hurt at first, but after a week or so I realized I should have admitted to myself long ago that our values and ideas about life were not compatible. I shall miss the company, but not the increasing misgivings about him."

When you do discover someone you like, even though you might think that you should marry right away because you are older and don't have much time, take at least a year or longer to spend as much time with that person to find out if you are truly compatible. Her are a few things to think about:

— Do you have fun and laugh?
— Do you share similar values and outlook on life?
— Do you like to share the same food and/or activities?
— How does the person treat his or her children and friends, and your family?
— Does he or she treat you and others with respect and kindness?
— Does the person spend more than he or she has, or, on the other hand, is cheap and miserly?
— Do you both like to read and/or watch television, or would you both rather be out doing some other activity?
— Does he or she have an uncontrollable temper?
— Does he or she constantly talk about himself or herself to the exclusion of others and/or you?
— Are you both in reasonably good health?
— Are you both talkers? Listeners? Or do you have real give and take conversations?
— Is the person too much older or younger than you are, running the risk that one of you will be left alone again, or have the responsibility of caring for the other?

If you find the answers to the above questions, and others you think of, are positive, great. Consider a long term commitment, and, when you do, consider having a party including family and friends so they can get to know your intended and each other.

You may be surprised at your children's reaction to your plan to remarry. Some children will be supportive, especially if they like your new companion, and will be happy for you. Other children may be upset, sometimes because they think you are being disloyal to their deceased parent, or because they are worried about an expected inheritance when you die.

For instance, Janice told me, "When my grandmother died after a long illness, my grandfather, who was 79, married the care giver who had helped him take care of his wife. At the time I was living fairly close to my grandfather and, one day, he came to see me to introduce his new wife.

"I am so happy for you," she said to her grand father, when he came into the kitchen to help her with the dishes after dinner. "Not everyone thinks our marriage was a good idea," he whispered with a frown. "My daughters, your aunts, are very upset. They think I married someone, in their words, "beneath my station". I also suspect they wonder what I will do with my estate. So thank you for your blessing. It means a lot to me."

"I couldn't help but wonder how my mother, who had died some years before and who was the peacemaker among her sisters, would have viewed my grandfather's remarriage."

The reason I tell you the above story is to urge you to take into consideration any concerns your children may have, but not to let them make your decision about remarrying.

If, after spending a good deal of time with a person, you find reasons that he or she is not what you want for a long term relationship, tell her or him, gently but firmly, and move on. Remaining friends is an option, but often if you are not compatible for the long term, a casual friendship will often wane, too. And remember, the other person was judging you, too. You may find that a companionship you thought was good isn't right for the other person. If so, be gracious and understanding, even if you are disappointed. Don't press for another chance, don't cry, don't be angry; just walk away. Life has setbacks, but how you deal with them is what will determine whether you are happy or sad.

**Give romance a chance,**
**But be cautious.**

# CONCLUSION

Whether we recognize it or not, each of us is special. We each bring to this world our individual talent, and education, and expertise, and memories, and passions, and yes, prejudices. **No** other person is exactly like **you**. When you live with another, often your focus is on the experiences and goals you share, while your own desires take second place or are forgotten. When you are left alone it is time to identify the wants, passions, and needs that will make your life feel fulfilled.

Remember, you are the captain in charge of your destiny, as well as the crew. Only you can make your life contented with moments of joy and even happiness. You must determine your destination and chart your course, then swab the decks, trim the sails and bail like crazy when you encounter turbulent seas. And whether you reach your goal or occasionally run aground, you must congratulate yourself or push the ship off the reef and set a new destination.

Of course, there will be times when you sorely miss your companion. This is natural. But keep your reminiscences positive and short. Instead, focus on making your life and thoughts positive, full of activity and laughter, and always looking to the future.

Please note that reading this book may not be the only assistance you need to learn to live alone successfully. I encourage you to seek other help. Help can be as simple as talking with someone else who lost a partner and has successfully gone on with his or her life. Maybe a group of widows or older singles would help you by talking about their problems; it is often encouraging to know other people have the same concerns and challenges as you. Community and senior centers, churches and funeral homes often offer or can recommend group therapy or counseling for survivors.

If none of the foregoing resources are available or do not appeal to you, or if you continue to feel angry, apathetic, or critical of others and/or your circumstances, call your health care provider for referrals to local support groups and professional help, or ask friends who have lost loved ones for a referrals to therapists they trust. Be sure to interview these professionals until you find one you like. Also, contact your health insurance company to find out if it will pay for therapy and/or be willing to recommend a therapist.

My hope is that this book has helped you to start on the path to a fulfilling life on your own. If you have comments, criticisms or suggestions, please email me at livalone@comcast.net. In any event, you will find me living alone but not lonely.

Remember:

**Living Alone Does Not Mean Lonely Living**